*I*T *T*A K E S *T*W O

L I F E ' S G O L D E N R U L E S™

IT TAKES TWO

The Golden Rules for Marital Bliss

GENERAL PUBLISHING GROUP
Los Angeles

The Life's Golden Rules series is published by General Publishing Group, Inc, 3100 Airport
Avenue, Santa Monica, CA 90405, 310-915-9000.

Library Catalog Number 93-079387
ISBN 1-881649-20-2

10 9 8 7 6 5 4 3 2 1

Quay Hays, Editor
Design by Deborah Daly
PRINTED IN THE USA

To

Sharon

SPOUSE

PARTNER

FRIEND

I T   T AKES   T WO

1 ♥ It's not the wedding, but everything that comes after that counts.

2 ♥ Marriage is two lives becoming one life remaining two lives.

3 ♥ If you married someone to change them,
    you married the wrong person.

4 ♥ Share secrets with one another.

5 ♥ Be on each other's side.

6 ♥ Don't expect your spouse to meet all of your needs. Meet your own.

7 ♥ Marriages made in Heaven are not exported.

8 ♥ It's okay to fight if you both fight fair.

9 ♥ Learn to forgive.

10 ♥ Try to communicate instead of just talk.

11 ♥ Share your toys.

12 ♥ Hold hands.

13 ♥ When your spouse is angry, keep calm. When one becomes fire, the other must be water.

14 ♥ Anger is okay—hostility is not.

15 ♥ The anger of lovers renews the strength of love.

16 ♥ Bottled up anger will fester and boil over.

17 ♥ Say, "I love you," right now.

18 ♥ Don't compare your spouse to someone else's.

19 ♥ You'll feel better when you say "I'm sorry" and mean it.

20 ♥ Have respect for the relationship.

21 ♥ Seek out adventures with your mate.

22 ♥ Be receptive to experimenting sexually
with each other.

23 ♥ Don't consider your marriage a failure
whenever it falls below a perfect score.

24 ♥ Remember that the grass is not always
greener on the other side.

25 ♥ Decide who takes care of bugs and spiders in the house.

26 ♥ Know where the line is drawn and never cross it.

27 ♥ Hurtful words and deeds leave permanent scars.

28 ♥ A long-term marriage has to move beyond chemistry—to compatibility, to friendship, to companionship.

29 ♥ There is little worse than forgetting important
dates—especially Valentine's Day!

30 ♥ Valentine's Day isn't the only time to
send flowers.

31 ♥ Put thought into gift-giving.

32 ♥ Don't wait until the last minute to buy a gift.

33 ♥ Don't expect your wife to be like your mother.

34 ♥ Your husband is not your father.

35 ♥ "Husbands are like fires—they go out when
unattended." – Zsa Zsa Gabor

36 ♥ The same goes for wives.

37 ♥ Trust.

38 ♥ Work at your marriage just like you work at your job.

39 ♥ Avoidance and withdrawal are danger signs. Make an effort to communicate instead.

40 ♥ Don't give up, get counseling.

41 ♥ Cuddle in bed.

42 ♥ Sleep naked on occasion.

43 ♥ Talk openly about sex.

44 ♥ Exercise together.

45 ♥ Agree to agree.

46 ♥ Don't criticize or argue in public.

47 ♥ Learn what not to say.

48 ♥ Include your spouse in your plans.

49 ♥ Always remember your marriage vows—
to love, honor and cherish.

50 ♥ Marriages are like gardens. Tend to them
and they thrive. Neglect them and they die.

51 ♥ Watch old Tracy and Hepburn films, but remember—they are only movies.

52 ♥ Don't judge your spouse until you judge yourself.

53 ♥ Try to understand what makes your
     partner tick.

54 ♥ Give compliments.

55 ♥ "Marriage is not just spiritual communion and passionate embraces; marriage is also three meals a day and remembering to carry out the trash."

—Dr. Joyce Brothers

56 ♥ Respect each other's privacy.

57 ♥ Learn to share the bathroom.

58 ♥ Put the toilet seat down.

59 ♥ A successful marriage requires falling in
    love several times—with the same person.

60 ♥ Take each other on a date at least once a week.

61 ♥ Whisper "dirty nothings" in his ear.

62 ♥ Remember your mother-in-law's
birthday.

63 ♥ Make sure you both agree on whether or
not you want children.

64 ♥ Discuss priorities.

65 ♥ Pursue your own interests.

66 ♥ Support each other's endeavors—
   indifference can be hurtful.

67 ♥ Emotions know no logic.

68 ♥ Jealousy is a wasted emotion.

69 ♥ Be friends.

70 ♥ "The great secret of a successful
marriage is to treat all disasters
as incidents, and none of the
incidents as disasters."

—Harold Nicolson, British Politician

71 ♥ Make mutual friends.

72 ♥ Accept each other's friends. Even if you don't like them, respect the friendship.

73 ♥ And try to be polite even if you don't like each other's friends.

74 ♥ It's nice to have someone to worry
about you. Don't fight it.

75 ♥ Find comfort in the fact that you're
not alone.

76 ♥ Be kind to each other.

77 ♥ Ask questions—don't interrogate.

78 ♥ Accusations usually backfire.

79 ♥ Explanations are much better than excuses.

80 ♥ The more you insist, the more your
   spouse will resist.

81 ♥ Never abuse one another.

82 ♥ Take a Time-Out when needed.

83 ♥ Don't be threatened by your spouse's
success. Enjoy it.

84 ♥ It's worth the effort to build a strong
foundation.

85 ♥ Renew your sex life often.

86 ♥ When you marry a person, you marry their
family as well.

87 ♥ "In a marriage there must be a readiness to accept the other person's tender spots, and accept loving gestures, touches and kindness. Shed the armor."

—Dr. Ruth

88 ♥ It's your job to not let your spouse drink and drive.

89 ♥ Call if you're going to be late.

90 ♥ It's not necessary to see the world from
your spouse's viewpoint. What's important
is to respect it.

91 ♥ Be considerate of each other's idiosyncrasies.

92 ♥ "Work out your Ying and Yang."

—Carl Jung

93 ♥ Don't run away from a crisis.

94 ♥ Listen, then talk.

95 ♥ Say nice things about your spouse to
   other people.

96 ♥ Buy presents your spouse—not you—
would like.

97 ♥ If one of you gets sick, make chicken
noodle soup.

98 ♥ Talk about your intimate life with your
spouse to friends and it's no longer intimate.

99 ♥ When you cheat on your spouse, you
cheat yourself.

100 ♥ Lies are a good marriage's worst enemy.

101 ♥ Buy sexy lingerie.

102 ♥ Do things together.

103 ♥ Go on business trips with each other
   when possible.

104 ♥ Take a bubble bath together.

105 ♥ Correct yourself, not your spouse.

106 ♥ Be clear and assertive when discussing money with your mate.

107 ♥ Always give your spouse a second chance.

108 ♥ Everything is forgivable.

109 ♥ Be loyal.

110 ♥ After you've tried everything, try one
more time.

111 ♥ Share responsibilities.

112 ♥ Don't do anything that would cause your
spouse to lose respect for you.

113 ♥ Don't embarrass each other.

114 ♥ Total predictability is one step away from monotony.

115 ♥ Give each other massages.

116 ♥ Frequent a favorite restaurant together.

117 ♥ Be your own person so you can be the
best person for your partner.

118 ♥ Be receptive, not defensive.

119 ♥ Teach each other new things.

120 ♥ Be known as a good listener.

121 ♥ Let up when it's not getting you anywhere.

122 ♥ Don't harp on the same things over and over and over again.

123 ♥ "Let your love be stronger than
your hate or anger. Learn the
wisdom of compromise, for it is
better to bend a little than to
break."

—Oscar Wilde

124 ♥ Compromise is the mother's milk of
marital longevity.

125 ♥ Read *Men Are From Mars, Women Are
From Venus.*

126 ♥ Anticipate the future.

127 ♥ Let each other sleep late.

128 ♥ Don't be too needy.

129 ♥ Control your temper.

130 ♥ It's silly to become enemies over
little things.

131 ♥ It doesn't matter who gets the last word.

132 ♥ "Never go to bed mad. Stay up
and fight."

—Phyllis Diller

133 ♥ Cook together.

134 ♥ Grow in love.

135 ♥ Marriage is like an edifice that must be
reinforced every day.

136 ♥ Where there's marriage without love,
     there will be love without marriage.

137 ♥ Love is love's reward.

138 ♥ Sympathize.

139 ♥ Take a deep breath before you criticize.

140 ♥ Try to be tolerant.

141 ♥ Humor has saved a lot of marriages.

142 ♥ Protect each other.

143 ♥ Call each other endearing names.

144 ♥ Sometimes it's important to give of
yourself even when you don't feel like it.

145 ♥ Count your blessings.

146 ♥ Intimacy in marriage is not just having sex—
   it's touching, talking, sharing and holding.

147 ♥ Value family heirlooms.

148 ♥ Renew your vows every ten years.

149 ♥ Read the Sunday paper together.

150 ♥ Take a class together.

151 ♥ Dance.

152 ♥ Don't envy your friends. You never know what goes on behind closed doors.

153 ♥ Talk about your beliefs.

154 ♥ Practice religious traditions.

155 ♥ Make holidays special for each other.

156 ♥ You want a good marriage.
Create it.

157 ♥ Share your fantasies.

158 ♥ Work together to create the family you want.

159 ♥ Aspire to no less than creating a long
marriage which will produce generations
that will make history.

160 ♥ Make your marriage your number
one priority.

161 ♥ Respect each other's opinions.

162 ♥ Write her a love letter.

163 ♥ Give time and space to your partner at
the end of the day.

164 ♥ "Let there be spaces in your togetherness."

—Kahlil Gibran, The Prophet

165 ♥ Agree on who balances the checkbook.

166 ♥ Decide together where to spend your money.

167 ♥ Don't be stingy.

168 ♥ Save, save, save.

169 ♥ Actions speak louder than words.

170 ♥ Don't assume, ask.

171 ♥ Your spouse is not to blame for your
weaknesses or failings.

172 ♥ "A good marriage is that in
which each appoints the other
the guardian of his solitude."

—Rainer Maria Rilke

173 ♥ Make intimacy a goal.

174 ♥ Try not to keep each other waiting.

175 ♥ If the interference of parents or inlaws in
your problems is unwanted, put a stop to it
quickly and firmly.

176 ♥ A spouse is not a housekeeper—but a partner.

177 ♥ Never forget that wives who work in the house and raise children—work!

178 ♥ Growth and change are part of marriage. Be thankful for them.

179 ♥ It is never okay to stray.

180 ♥ If the fire goes out, rekindle it.

181 ♥ "In a successful marriage, there is no such thing as one's way. There is only the way of both, only the bumpy, dusty, difficult, but always mutual paths." —Phyllis McGinley

182 ♥ No one said it would be easy.

183 ♥ A good marriage is worth fighting for.

184 ♥ Never swear at each other.

185 ♥ When you entertain, help each other out.

186 ♥ You marry a person, not a god.

187 ♥ Set your priorities in order.

188 ♥ You are not your spouse's "ex." Do not
make or allow comparisons.

189 ♥ Stepchildren can enrich your lives, but
they shouldn't dominate them.

190 ♥ Say good morning and good night.

191 ♥ Give privacy in the bathroom.

192 ♥ Do little favors for each other.

193 ♥ Keep your values intact.

194 ♥ You can find your voice in the bedroom
  just as well as in the board room.

195 ♥ Love grows with kindness.

196 ♥ Like the person you marry.

197 ♥ Create new dreams together.

198 ♥ Boredom starts with boring people.

199 ♥ Men and women sometimes look at emotional issues differently.

200 ♥ Husbands are not just "daddies."

201 ♥ Seek higher understanding of your problems.

202 ♥ "Marriage is popular because it combines the maximum of temptation with the maximum of opportunity."

—George Bernard Shaw

203 ♥ Life is filled with everyday stresses.
It's how you handle these stresses together
that's important.

204 ♥ Don't eat crackers in bed.

205 ♥ Spend quality time with your partner.

206 ♥ Never take your marriage for granted.

207 ♥ Never take your spouse for granted.

208 ♥ Your partner's past is past. Your future
is your future.

209 ♥ Marriage helps you grow up.

210 ♥ Life is not always fair, and neither
is marriage.

211 ♥ "By all means marry. If you get a good wife, you will become very happy; if you get a bad one, you will become a philosopher—and that is good for every man."

—Socrates, philosopher

212 ♥ To create lasting human love, begin
with romantic love.

213 ♥ There are no princes on white horses.
Only real men in cars.

214 ♥ Hold your marriage in high esteem.

215 ♥ Have long conversations.

216 ♥ Take walks together.

217 ♥ Marriages do not fail, people do.

218 ♥ Mind, not body, makes marriage lasting.

219 ♥ Don't let others meddle in your marriage.

220 ♥ Ask people who have been married many years for advice—not friends who are single.

221 ♥ Marry to please yourself, not others.

222 ♥ Marry because you want to, not because you have to.

223 ♥ Marriage is. . ."A book in which the first chapter is written in poetry and the remaining chapters in prose."

—Beverly Nichols

224 ♥ There is no definition of marriage.
Each couple creates its own meaning.

225 ♥ It's better to be married and sometimes
miserable, than miserable and always alone.

226 ♥ Marriage is. . . "That relation between man and woman in which the independence is equal, the dependence mutual, and the obligation reciprocal."

—Louis K. Anspacher

227 ♥ People may joke about marriage, but
it is the way of mankind.

228 ♥ Marriage is habit forming. Just make sure
they're good habits.

229 ♥ A good marriage is greater than the
sum of its parts.

230 ♥ Marriage is a shared past and
        lasting memories.

231 ♥ Married people can become better
        people together.

232 ♥ Be sincere.

233 ♥ Never betray your partner's confidence.

234 ♥ Eat by candlelight.

235 ♥ Think about the other person.

236 ♥ Think each other is deserving.

237 ♥ It takes two—working together for marital bliss.

238 ♥ Decide how you both want to discipline
    your children.

239 ♥ Don't involve your children in your problems.

240 ♥ Make a home.

241 ♥ Remain a united front.

242 ♥ PMS is a fact of life. Be understanding.

243 ♥ Make sure you remind each other to go
to the doctor.

244 ♥ Bite your tongue when he wears an outfit
that doesn't match.

245 ♥ Do something wild and crazy.

246 ♥ Acknowledge each other's feelings.

247 ♥ Expect the unexpected.

248 ♥ You only "nag" the ones you love.

249 ♥ Take a bike ride together.

250 ♥ Don't throw out his old high school trophies.

251 ♥ Take lots of pictures.

252 ♥ Share your ice cream cone.

253 ♥ Don't play partners with your spouse in tennis.

254 ♥ The same goes for Bridge.

255 ♥ Be accepting of each other's faults.

256 ♥ Take lots of pictures.

257 ♥ Know when you're in a no-win situation.

258 ♥ Back off when tempers flare.

259 ♥ Take care of each other's hurts.

260 ♥ Always have a bottle of champagne chilled for special occasions.

261 ♥ Create mystique.

262 ♥ Flirt with each other.

263 ♥ "A marriage is like a long trip in a rowboat. If one passenger starts to row the boat, the other has to steady it; otherwise they will go to the bottom."

—David Reuben

264 ♥ Listen to Simon and Garfunkel's
      "Bridge Over Troubled Water."

265 ♥ See the movie, *Much Ado About Nothing*.

266 ♥ Memorize the chorus to "Lean on Me."

267 ♥ Be supportive of your wife's career.

268 ♥ Don't cancel out each other's vote.

269 ♥ Remain an individual.

270 ♥ Pick up your clothes.

271 ♥ Bring breakfast in bed.

272 ♥ Know your wife's favorite perfume and
buy it when you see she's running out.

273 ♥ Let tragedy strengthen, not divide you.

274 ♥ Know how far you can push.

275 ♥ If you change the rules in your marriage,
change them together.

276 ♥ Kiss good morning.

277 ♥ Never end the courtship.

278 ♥ Always kiss each other goodbye.

279 ♥ If you have love, you
have everything.

280 ♥ Don't go through your husband's pockets
or your wife's purse.

281 ♥ Buy special greeting cards every so often.

282 ♥ Leave sexy messages for each other on
the answering service.

283 ♥ When you love, you both become
  beautiful to each other.

284 ♥ Love, and you shall be loved.

285 ♥ "The love you take is equal to
the love you make."

—Lennon and McCartney

286 ♥ If tan legs turn him on, get a little sun.

287 ♥ If beards turn her on, grow one.

288 ♥ Make little changes if they'll help.

289 ♥ Stay away from things that go against your
nature.

290 ♥ You can't solve every problem
each other has.

291 ♥ Do not lecture.

292 ♥ Don't push "hot" buttons.

293 ♥ Look for mutual solutions with which
you can both be satisfied.

294 ♥ Holding grudges returns too little results
for the amount of effort required.

295 ♥ Make healthy meals.

296 ♥ Learn from each other.

297 ♥ Don't be "so" literal.

298 ♥ Learn to take a joke.

299 ♥ Go to a museum together.

300 ♥ Love yourself and only then can you
love each other.

301 ♥ Say thank you.

302 ♥ Break old destructive patterns.

303 ♥ You don't have to like the same things.

304 ♥ Debate—don't bicker.

305 ♥ Watch your tone of voice.

306 ♥ Don't always have the "brakes" on.

307 ♥ Give 110% to your marriage.

308 ♥ Always try to look your best for
your spouse.

309 ♥ Give suggestions when asked.

310 ♥ You can each change in positive ways
    if you want to.

311 ♥ Write a poem for her birthday.

312 ♥ Ask your mate if you want to celebrate
birthdays that end in zero.

313 ♥ Leave notes on important dates in
   each other's calendars.

314 ♥ Don't patronize your mate.

315 ♥ Call each other during the day.

316 ♥ Read the cartoon "Love is. . ."

317 ♥ Read each other's horoscope.

318 ♥ It doesn't matter who goes first.

319 ♥ "You can't always get what
you want."

—Jagger/Richard

320 ♥ Videotape your wedding and watch it
together on a slow night.

321 ♥ Keep each other safe.

322 ♥ Don't make jokes at your spouse's
expense.

323 ♥ Don't give orders.

324 ♥ Marital bliss comes in starts and stops.

325 ♥ Play hookey together.

326 ♥ Keep each other's picture in your wallet.

327 ♥ Don't forget that today is what happens
while you're busy making other plans.

328 ♥ "Love is not a matter of counting the years, it's making the years count."

—W. Smith

329 ♥ Ask your spouse to help you with
your work projects.

330 ♥ Go shopping together to learn what
each other likes.

331 ♥ Help out with chores.

332 ♥ Don't ever ignore one another.

333 ♥ Encourage—don't discourage.

334 ♥ Don't get defensive when your spouse
     tries to teach you something new.

335 ♥ No one is right all the time.

336 ♥ Treat each other as life-long companions.

337 ♥ Spend a romantic night at a nearby hotel.

338 ♥ Use team-work in all things.

339 ♥ Fight for each other's rights.

340 ♥ Make a plan together.

341 ♥ Be patient.

342 ♥ Remember that worrying won't
    solve anything.

343 ♥ Don't hold on to negative issues.

344 ♥ Buy life insurance.

345 ♥ Explore new places together.

346 ♥ Discuss current events regularly.

347 ♥ Don't repeat negative patterns.

348 ♥ Everyone has flaws—no one is perfect.

349 ♥ Share Superbowl Sunday together.

350 ♥ Get involved in a charity together.

351 ♥ Read a book together.

352 ♥ Remember that every mid-life doesn't
     need to have a crisis.

353 ♥ Time heals many wounds.

354 ♥ Take some vacations without the kids.

355 ♥ Take care of your health.

356 ♥ You get out of a marriage what you put into it.

357 ♥ Find common interests.

358 ♥ Compromise on how hot or cold to
keep the house.

359 ♥ Turn the lights off.

360 ♥ Marriage is a fan club with only two fans.

361 ♥ Keep remembering the qualities you
   admire in the other person.

362 ♥ Sometimes you have to throw logic
out the door.

363 ♥ Separate current problems from
past problems.

364 ♥ The healthiest relationship is
a partnership of equals.

365 ♥ Say, "I love you" . . . again.

<u>Favorites</u>

1.

2.

3.

4.

5.

6.